Robert Barnes

English Lutheran Martyr

"Our good, pious table companion and guest of our home, this holy martyr, St. Robertus"—Luther

by
William Dallmann

◆ REPRISTINATION PRESS ◆
MALONE, TEXAS

Originally published by Concordia Publishing House. Now in the public domain.
1997 edition published by Repristination Press. Reprinted in 2012.

◆REPRISTINATION PRESS◆
P.O. Box 173
Bynum, Texas 76631
www.repristinationpress.com

ISBN 1891469029

Table of Contents

FOREWORD.

Some years ago the writer had a sketch of Robert Barnes in *The Theological Quarterly* and later he revised it for *The Walther League Messenger*. It seems no one ever brought out the martyr's life in a book. The writer thinks it should be done, and he has done it. It should be interesting especially to English speaking Lutherans to know how Lutheranism came to the English speaking people.

Hearty thanks are hereby given to Professor Pardieck and Pastor Herman W. Meyer for transcribing a reference; to Professor Fuerbringer and Union Seminary for the loan of rare books; to Dr. Preserved Smith for valuable references, some of which could be used, though the work was already in type.

That the reader may get a little of the pleasure and profit the writer had in getting out this labor of love, is the hope of

THE AUTHOR.

ROBERT BARNES
Luther's English Friend

I.
Barnes at Cambridge.

Robert Barnes was born in 1495 near Lynn, in Norfolk, England, and at an early age became an Augustinian monk at Cambridge.

Showing a taste for learning, he was sent to the University of Louvain, and on his return, about 1523, was made prior of the convent. He "caused the house shortly to flourish with good letters, and made a great part of the house learned who before were drowned in barbarous ignorance." They read Cicero, Terence, Plautus, and the Epistles of St. Paul.

II.
Luther's Books Come to England.

Luther nailed his famous Ninety-five Theses to the Wittenberg Castle Church on October 31, 1517, "and in two years from that day, there was scarcely perhaps a village from the Irish Channel to the Danube in which the name of Luther was not familiar as a word of hope and promise," writes Froude. As early as 1520 the learned Italian bishop Polydore Vergil speaks of the importation into England of a great number of "Lutheran books."

The new learning was fanatically opposed. As Tyndale puts it, "the barking curs, Duns' disciples, the children of darkness, raged in every pulpit against Greek, Latin, and Hebrew."

Visiting the continent in July, 1520, King Henry received Erasmus, who talked of writing against Luther. Pope Leo X ordered Cardinal Wolsey to burn Luther's books.

In March 1521 Archbishop Warham of London wrote Cardinal Wolsey some of Oxford were infected with the, "heresyes of Luther . . . the heryng whereof should be right delectable and pleasant to open Lutheranes beyond the see," and asked for an investigation. Within fifteen days "all writings and books of Martin Luther, the heretic," were to be given up under penalty of death by burning. On May 12, 1521, Bishop Fisher of Rochester preached at St. Paul's Church "Against ye pernicious doctryn of Martin Luther."

King Henry, Cardinal Wolsey, the foreign ambassadors, and others witnessed the burning of Luther's books. Henry asked Duke Louis of Bavaria to go the limit against Luther.

At Wolsey's desire Henry himself dipped his loyal pen into the royal ink pot and wrote "An Assertion of the Seven Sacraments against Martin Luther," London, July, 1521. How did he write? "What pest so pernicious... What pest so poisonous? ... What wolf of hell is he! What a limb of Satan! How rotten is his mind!"

Henry dedicated his work to the pope. Leo was so tickled that he entitled the King "Defender of the Faith," and granted all readers an indulgence for ten years and ten periods of forty days.

On October 27, 1521, Richard Pace wrote Cardinal Wolsey: "Itt is to Hys Graces grete contentacion and comforte to have understonde att large Popis Holynesse haith acceptidde hys bokes wretyn agaynst Luther."

Luther paid the royal ruffian in like coin and with compound interest.

Henry asked the rulers of Saxony to put down "that execrable sect of Luther . . . with blood, if it cannot be done otherwise." Bishop Fisher also again attacked Luther: "A Confutation of the Lutheran Assertion," 1523; "Defense of the Christian Priesthood," 1524; "Defense of King Henry's 'Assertion of the Seven Sacraments'," 1525. This good soul could not understand how such fine Lutheran books could come from heretics. It is strange, isn't it? This best and most learned of the English bishops could write: "Now Luther is become a big fox.... What do I say? . . . a fox? He is a mad dog, a ravening wolf, a cruel bear, or rather all those animals in one; for the monster includes many beasts within him."

The holy Sir Thomas More preached beautifully on liberty in *Utopia*, but in England he most cruelly persecuted the Lutherans and he attacked Luther in the vilest manner, using unspeakably filthy language. Though More's friend and Luther's enemy, Erasmus was offended at More's billingsgate.

Thomas Bilney read the New Testament and Luther's books and had a religious experience much like Luther's. Little Bililey brought Luther's books to the knowledge of Barnes, and the Prior became an ardent follower of the great Reformer.

When Hugh Latimer would take a degree, he attacked "Philip Melanchthon and his Opinions." Little Bilney went to Latimer's room and from that time forward Latimer "began to smell the Word of God, and forsook the school-doctors and such fooleries."

Bilney and Latimer visited the foul hospitals and foul jails and distributed food; Bilney ate but one meal a day—"Saint" Bilney.

Nicholas Ridley was another, later burned with Hugh Latimer.

George Stafford introduced lecturing on the Bible. He visited one Sir Henry, the conjurer, sick of the plague, brought him to repentance, and caused all his conjuring books to be burned before his face; but Stafford was infected himself and died.

Thomas Allen, son of the Lord Mayor of London, was another; he comforted Saint Bilney when burnt at the stake. Rudolph Bradford, later exiled for spreading the New Testament, was another of the band; so was Sygar Nicholson, later cruelly treated for having Luther's works in his house.

Another was Miles Coverdale, later Bishop of Exeter, who was twice pastor of Bergzabern in Zweibruecken, and received his degree of Doctor of Divinity from Tuebingen. He published "Biblia. The Bible, that is the Holy Scriptures of the Olde and New Testament, faithfully and truly translated out of Douche and Latyn into Englishe," 1535. He translated hymns of Luther and others in the original meter, which were sung to the Lutheran melodies: the first English hymn-book was a Lutheran one. It was known as the "Goostly Psalmes and Spirituall Songes drawen out of the Holy Scripture for the comforte and consolacyon of such as loue to rcioyce in God and his Worde." In Germany he was known as Michael Anglus. He married the sister of the wife of McAlpine, Dr. Macchabaeus, the Scotch translator of the Danish Bible.

These first English Lutherans, twenty-seven of whom are known by name, often met in "The White Horse," because they could come in privately by the back door. They were called "Germans," and the house "Germany," because there they studied the works of Luther, and where they took their walks was known as "Heretics' Hill."

Thomas Cranmer also remained at Cambridge and studied the Bible and Luther's books, and about 1525 began to pray privately for the end of the pope's power in England. For sixteen years he remained at Jesus College, built on the nunnery of St. Rhadegunde, which had been suppressed for gross immorality.

III.
English Lutherans Teach at Oxford.

About 1524 Cardinal Wolsey suppressed twenty-two smaller monasteries for their immorality and with the funds, about 8,000 Pounds—$100,000—founded the splendid Cardinal College at Oxford, now known as Christ Church College, and called a number of bright young Cambridge men as teachers.

As a result of the labors of the new professors, "Lutheranism increased daily in the University of Oxford.... Many eminent men did dispute and preach in the University against it, yet the Lutherans proceeded, and took all private occasions to promote their doctrine."

Warham again wrote Wolsey "With respect to the most accursed works of Luther," and Wolsey called it the "hellish Lutheran heresy."

Among these bright young professors was John Frith, who helped William Tyndale translate the Bible, was imprisoned in the fish cellar of the College, was released, went to Marburg in Hessen, met Patrick Hamilton, and translated his "Places." He was burnt at Smithfield on July 4, 1533.

Another was Richard Taverner, a layman who preached in the streets and catechized children. He translated the Augsburg Confession in 1536, got out the English Bible in 1539 and two editions of the New Testament and a book of sermons in two parts in 1540.

Richard Cox was later tutor to King Edward VI, Chancellor of the University, one of the compilers of the "Book of Common Prayer," exiled under "Bloody Mary."

"The chiefest Lutheran at this time was John Clark. So great a respect had they for his doctrine and exemplary course of life, that they would often recur to him for resolution of doubts. They also had their private meetings, wherein they conferred about the promotion of their religion. They prayed together and read certain books containing the principles of Luther."

"The Association of Christian Brothers" was formed in London about 1525—poor men, chiefly laborers, and a very few of the clergy. They went up and down the country selling Tyndale's New Testament and translations of Luther's works. This was heresy, and, of course, they risked their lives. One of these was Thomas Garrett, a fellow of Magdalen College and curate of All Hallows church in London. He came to Oxford and sold Lutheran books to the students.

Detectives were sent to arrest him, but Arthur Cole, an old college mate, warned him. Anthony Dalaber helped him to escape, but Garrett was arrested at Dover and given over to Cardinal Wolsey. All were thrown into prison. Some were exiled. Clark "died in August, 1528, of a distemper occasioned by the stench of the prison in which he was confined." So did Sumner.

Bishop Stokesley of London said it was "abusing the people to give them liberty to read the Scriptures." And the great and "good" Thomas More called it "a design to depreciate the authority of an ordained priesthood and of an organized Church." Quite true, the Bible and the Roman Church do not get on very well.

This is the way the bishops looked at them in 1529—"In the crime of heresy, thanked be God, there hath no notable person fallen in our time. . . . Truth it is that certain apostate friars and monks, lewd priests, bankrupt merchants, vagabonds and lewd idle fellows of corrupt nature, have embraced the abominable and erroneous opinions lately sprung up in Germany, and by them have been some seduced in simplicity and ignorance. Against these, if judgment have been exercised according to the law of the realm, we be without blame. If we have been too remiss or slack, we shall gladly do our duty henceforth."

They surely did their "duty." By the act of Henry V, every officer, from the lord chancellor to the parish constable, was sworn to seek them out and destroy them; and both bishops and officials had shown no reluctance to execute their duty. Hunted like wild beasts from hiding-place to hiding-place, decimated by the stake, beset by informers, imprisoned, racked, and scourged, worst of all, haunted by their own infirmities, the flesh shrinking before the dread of a death of agony—thus it was that they struggled on; earning for themselves martyrdom,—for **us**, the free England in which we live and breathe, writes Froude.

IV.
Barnes Is Tried.

At Cambridge Barnes discussed matters of theology and in 1523 became a Doctor of Divinity. Returning from the continent, on Sunday, Dec. 24, 1525, he reproduced Luther's sermon for the fourth Sunday in Advent on Phil. 4:4 in St. Edward's Church at Cambridge, and also made a bold attack on the extravagance of Cardinal Wolsey. He was accused of heresy. He promised to make answer at the next convocation. Dr. Nottoris begged him to recant, but Barnes was steadfast.

Six days before Shrovetide Master Gibson, a London sergeant-at-arms, came to Cambridge and suddenly arrested Dr. Barnes openly in the convocation house, to make all others afraid, and made search for Luther's books and all the German works. But Dr. Forman of Queen's College had sent word to the rooms of the thirty suspected persons, and the books were hid.

The arrest of Dr. Barnes caused a great stir, the Lutheran doctrines were discussed with great heat, "one preaching against another." Barnes was taken to London, and the next day to Westminster, to the Pope's Legate, Cardinal Wolsey.

The magnificent Cardinal would know whether Barnes really thought all this grand display was wrong and that the money ought to be given to the poor "that will soon .... them out against the wall."

Yes, Barnes really thought so and again freely said so.

"Will you be ruled by us, and we will do all things for your honesty and for the honesty of your University."

"I thank your Grace for your good will. I will stick

to the Holy Scripture and to God's book, according to the simple talent that God hath lent me."

"Well, thou shalt have thy learning tried to the uttermost, and thou shalt have the law."

Barnes was examined in February, 1526 by the bishops of London, Rochester, Bath, and St. Asaph's on twenty-five articles. Coverdale and two other Cambridge friends acted as his secretaries in preparing his reply.

As a result of the examination he was called on to turn or burn. Barnes was inclined to burn, but Gardiner, Wolsey's secretary, had known Barnes at Cambridge as "beloved of many as a good fellow in company," though "of a merry scoffing wit," and felt the duty to befriend him, and got him to swear off his teaching.

Barnes and four German merchants of the Steelyard, who had been condemned at the same time for spreading Luther's works, were sentenced to carry fagots at St. Paul's.

At eight o'clock in the morning of Shrove Sunday, Feb. 11, 1526, the cathedral was crowded; Cardinal Wolsey, with thirty-six abbots, mitred priors, and bishops, "in gowns of damask and satin," sat enthroned on a scaffold at the top of the stairs, "in Purple, euen like a bloudy Antichrist."

Bishop Fisher of Rochester stood in a new pulpit and preached from Luke 18:42, the lesson for *Quinquagesima*, "Against Luther and Dr. Barnes." He said: "To all them that be not ouer peruersedly drowned in the heresies of Luther it shall appare (as I verily suppose) that his doctryne is veray pestilent and pernitious."

Barnes, kneeling, asked forgiveness of God, the church, and the Cardinal. Hereupon he was led to the Rood of Northen, or crucifix at the north door of the cathedral, where a fire had been kindled, marched around it three times, threw in his five fagots, and thus helped burn "large basketfuls" of Luther's books and Tyndale's New Testament—at least Tyndale thought so. At last absolution was pronounced by Bishop Fisher, and Barnes was restored to the church.

V.
Barnes Flees to Germany.

Barnes was sent back to the Fleet and kept in prison half a year; afterwards he was "a free prisoner" in the Austin Friars in London. On fresh complaints he was sent to Northampton, where he once more stood in danger of burning as a relapsed heretic, most likely for selling a New Testament at Michaelmas, 1526. In the third year of his imprisonment, in 1528, he escaped to Antwerp and spent about three years in Germany under the name of Anthonius Amarius. He entered the University of Wittenberg under the name of Antonius Anglus, lived in Bugenhagen's house, made the acquaintance of Luther, even lodged with him, and obtained some influence with the Elector of Saxony and with King Frederick I of Denmark.

VI.
Barnes' Nineteen Theses.

In 1530 Barnes published at Wittenberg a defense of Lutheran teaching, for which Bugenhagen wrote a foreword. The theses are in substance: 1. Faith alone justifies. 2. Christ made satisfaction not alone for original sin, but for all sins. 3. The commandments of God cannot be observed from our own powers. 4. Free will of its own powers can do nothing but sin. 5. The righteous sin even in every good work. 6. The true marks of the Church. 7. The power of the keys depends upon the Word of God, and not upon man's power. 8. Councils can err. 9. Communion must be administered under both forms. 10. Human ordinances do not bind the conscience. 11. Auricular confession is not necessary to salvation. 12. It is lawful for priests to marry. 13. Monks are not holier than laymen. 14. Christian fasting does not consist in distinctions of meats. 15. Christians keep holy and worship God every day, and not only on the seventh. 16. Unjust Papal excommunication does not injure those against whom it is directed. 17. The true body of Christ is in the sacrament of the altar. 18. Saints are not to be invoked as mediators. 19. The errors of the Romish Mass are named. On Nov. 14, a copy was sent by Stephen Vaughan for presentation to King Henry.*

VII.
Lutherans Persecuted in England.

While Barnes was safe in Germany, his friend Thomas Bilney was arrested in 1529. Three times he refused to recant; the fourth time he fell. For two years he

---

* The title is *Sentenciae ex doctoribus collectae, quas papistae valde impudenter hodie damnant. Per Anto. Anglum. Wittebergae*—"Sentences collected from the Doctors (Church Fathers) which the Papists today very impudently condemn." It was printed by Joseph Clug. It is a pamphlet of 152 pages, 3 x 5¾. A fine copy is in the Union Seminary Library at New York City. Bugenhagen translated the work into German—*Furnehmlich Artikel der Christlichen Kirchen*, printed at Nuernberg, 1531. A copy is also at Union Seminary.

was miserable; "he would go up to Jerusalem"; he preached in the fields; he gave away a New Testament; he was burned by the Bishop of Norwich in 1531.

James Bainham, a lawyer, was arrested, racked by Sir Thomas More. Enfeebled by suffering, he recanted before the cold merciless eyes of Bishop Stokesley. His conscience troubled him. He went to the Christian Brothers and asked forgiveness.

He arose in church with the fatal English Testament in his hand and "declared openly, before all the people, with weeping tears, that he had denied God," praying them all to forgive him, and beware of his weakness; "for if I should not return to the truth, this Word of God would damn me, body and soul, at the day of judgment." Then he prayed "everybody rather to die than to do as he did, for he would not feel such a hell again as he did feel for all the world's good."

He was taken to Bishop Stokesley's coal cellar at Fulham, put into irons and the stocks, and left there for many days in the cold March weather to think it over. This failing to work conviction, he was dragged to Sir Thomas More's house at Chelsea, where for two nights he was chained to a post and whipped. He was returned to Fulham palace for another week of torture, then to the Tower for another two weeks' torture, again without avail. He was burned at Smithfield on the last of April, 1532.

VIII.
Henry Would Divorce Katherine.

When Henry VIII had no son by Catherine of Aragon, he sent Dr. Wm. Knight to get a papal permit to take a second wife, but withdrew the request before it was presented to Pope Clement VII; now Henry wanted a divorce. On Oct. 5, 1529, Ghinucci was sent to the Pope to maintain Henry's right to change his wives at his pleasure. Henry's agent, Sir Gregory Casale, or Cassell, wrote on Sept. 18, 1530, the Pope proposed Henry might have two wives, and the party of Kaiser Karl favored the plan, though Catherine was Karl's aunt.

Why not? Henry's brother-in-law, the Duke of Suffolk, had two living wives beside the King's sister—perfectly all right by papal permit. Why not? Henry's sister Margaret, Queen of Scotland, got a papal permit to divorce the Earl of Angus on such flimsy grounds that Henry had Wolsey write her about "the shameless sentence sent from Rome" and warn her of the "inevitable damnation of adulterers." Why not? The pope had given a permit to Louis XII of France to divorce his wife for reasons similar to Henry's.

Why not? A pope had allowed the same thing to a king of Castile not long before. Why not? Pope Clement VII himself had "two wives" with him when meeting King Francis I of France at Marseilles in November, 1535. And Cardinal Wolsey had more "wives." And Bishop Gardiner of Winchester carried "two wives" in male attire with him on his travels.

Cardinal Cajetan favored the plan of two wives for Henry, and so did Erasmus, the prince of scholars. Calvin advised that the queen be put away, and Zwingli thought the marriage should be dissolved.

When the powerful Wolsey was powerless to get Henry's divorce, he fell from power, and on his death bed wailed: "If I had served God so diligently as I have done the king, He would not have given me over in my gray hairs.

Howbeit, this is the just reward that I must receive for my worldly-diligence and pains that I had to do him service, only to satisfy his vain pleasure, not regarding my godly duty."

He also sent warning to Henry to "have a vigilant eye on the new sect, the Lutherans, that it do not increase through your negligence in such sort as you be at length compelled to put harness on your back to subdue them."

IX.
Henry Seeks Luther's Help.

As stated before, in 1521 King Henry had written against Luther in the most insulting manner, and Luther had replied in like language. In 1525, when King Christian II of Denmark told Luther the English King was favoring the Gospel, Luther put away all personal feeling and for the sake of the Gospel wrote Henry a most humble offer of reconciliation. To this Henry in August, 1526, replied more insultingly than he had written at first, and he put Luther and Kate into a farce with buffoons at his revels on St. Martin's Eve, Nov. 10, 1527, and scolded him for living with a nun. But he kept a private cabinet full of Lutheran books and read them with eagerness and intelligence, and in 1529 he highly praised Luther to Chapuys, Kaiser Karl's ambassador, and was very sorry he had ever written against him. The king even went so far as to publish a translation of Luther's letter of 1525 and to say he had been overpersuaded by Cardinal Wolsey to write against Luther! That comes pretty near being an apology from the English king to the German boor.

In 1530 Henry spent about 5,000 crowns sending

Cranmer to get the universities and the Protestants on the continent to support his divorce. He thought Cranmer "hath the right sow by the ear," or "hath the sow by the right ear." Either of these elegant versions makes clear the royal thought that Cranmer was on the right track to get Henry's divorce.

In 1531 Henry tried to win the Lutherans for his divorce. Simon Grynaeus, the Basel scholar, was to handle Melanchthon, but on August 23 Master Philip prepared an unfavorable reply. Henry sent William Paget to gain Luther. He came August 12, 1532, and applied to Barnes.

Luther would not consent to the divorce of the innocent queen.

"Since I can do nothing else, my prayer is directed to God that Christ may hinder this divorce and make void the counsels of Ahitophel in persuading it, and that the queen may have firm faith and constant assurance that she is and will be Queen of England, even though the gates of the world and of hell may oppose."

Luther's letter was dated Sept. 2. On the 4th Barnes left Wittenberg, went by way of Magdeburg and Luebeck, and came to London in December. Henry was angry at Luther's message, and dismissed the innocent messenger "with much ill will." In addition to this, the new chancellor, Sir Thomas More, would throw him into prison, but had to content himself with writing a bitter attack on him.

It seems during this time Barnes lived at the Steelyard in Thames Street, near London Bridge, the privileged house of the Hanse merchants, one prosperous German of whom was Georg Gisze, made immortal by Holbein's glorious portrait, admired so much by Ruskin. (The ancient place was pulled down in 1863 to make way for the South

Eastern Railway Station in Cannon Street.)

On June 16, 1533 Luther presided at a discussion of theses hurriedly prepared by Melanchthon when John Bugenhagen, Caspar Cruciger, and John Aepinus were made Doctors of Theology. The Englishman, Dr. Robert Barnes, and the Scot, Canon Alexander Alane, Alesius, took part in the disputation. The Elector John Frederick, his brother John Ernest, Dukes Francis of Lueneburg and Magnus of Mecklenburg, and other princely and great lords attended to the end. The Elector bore the costs of the promotion and also stood the doctor banquet in the Castle, where the guests filled eighteen to twenty tables.

At this time we find at the University the name of Antonius Anglus—"Barnes," Melanchthon wrote in the margin. For Alesius Luther and Melanchthon procured an income from the Elector.

Henry made another effort to win the Lutherans by sending over a young Englishman.

In July, 1533, Stephen Vaughan and Christopher Mont came to Nuernberg to learn the state of Germany as to religion and sent home reports. In January 1534, Christopher Mont and Nicholas Heath brought Henry's sympathy to the Lutheran princes as being also an enemy of the pope and expressed his willingness to unite with them to root out false doctrines.

In 1534 Barnes was sent by Henry to Hamburg, from which city he, on July 12, advised the King to abandon Luebeck and ally himself with Christian III, the newly elected King of Denmark. In August we find him back in England, in daily discussion with the bishops, no doubt defending the supremacy of the king over the pope.

On Henry's request the Hamburgers sent their

chief pastor, John Aepinus, to England to consult with the king on introducing the Reformation into England. He left on June 12, 1534, and returned in January, only after the Hamburgers had requested the king to release their pastor, since they needed his services.

On March 11, 1535, Barnes was once more in Wittenberg, "treating only of the second marriage of the king; but, as he says, the king has no concern for the affairs of the Church." Of course, he did not win over the Lutherans to the divorce.

He found them worked up over the news that Henry had killed Chancellor More and Bishop Fisher.

On Barnes' request Melanchthon on the 13th wrote Henry a letter. After some fulsome flattery he urges "a simple and sure form of doctrine," and "care ought to be taken that cruelty be not inflicted upon good men." To this letter Archbishop Laurence attributes the Articles of Faith published during Henry's reign. Barnes soon after returned to England.

On Barnes' suggestion also Melanchthon in August dedicated his Loci on the Epistle to the Romans to King Henry, not as a patron, but as a censor, and asked him to study and criticize the book! For this dedication Philip got two hundred crowns from "Your friend, King Henry VIII."

The work was taken to England by Alesius, whom John Stigelius "pursued with an elegy." This Alesius is the Canon Alex. Alane, who escaped to Wittenberg after the fiery death of Patrick Hamilton, Scotland's first Lutheran preacher and martyr.

Cromwell got him to dispute with Bishop Stokesly on the number of the sacraments, and Archbishop Cranmer entertained him at his palace at Lambeth.

In May or June Barnes and one Derick were sent to Germany. In this year King Henry calls Barnes *"Capellanum nostrum et S. Theologiae Professorem."*

X.
Barnes Arranges An Embassy.

In September Barnes was again sent to Wittenberg, this time in great haste. Why this haste? King Francis of France also played politics, and wished to join the Bund of Schmalkalden, and thus head the Protestants. For this purpose he and Cardinal Bellay invited Melanchthon to visit France, and Henry hastened to head off his good Catholic brother and rival. Melanchthon felt like visiting France, Luther favored-the plan, but the Elector very curtly forbade the visit.

Luther and others urged the Elector to give Barnes a hearing.

1. Would an embassy be received to confer with Luther?
2. Would Melanchthon visit England to confer with King Henry?
3. King Henry would join the Bund of Schmalkalden if given a place befitting his rank.

On September 21 the Elector answered.

1. An embassy would be received.
2. The question of Melanchthon's visit had to be deferred, though Luther favored the visit.
3. King Henry could join the Bund on heartily accepting the Augsburg Confession.

On the 26 the Elector gave Barnes a letter, urging Henry "to reform the doctrine of religion."

During this visit King Henry's chaplain, Dr. Barnes, attended another doctor promotion. Jerome Weller and Nicholas Medler were made doctors of theology. The disputation was held on Sept. 11, under the presidency of Luther as Dean, the promotion on the 14th under Cruciger, the promoter was Justus Jonas. The university had been sent to Jena, on account of the plague; but Melanchthon, Cruciger, Myconius, and Menius came over for the promotion. Besides there were present Bugenhagen, Amsdorf, Roerer, Hausmann, Jerome and Augustine Schurf, and, of course, the ambassador from England, Dr. Robert Barnes.

Kate Luther cooked the *"splendidum prandium"* for which Jonas had to get all kinds of fowl from Jena. Luther had begged the Elector to send venison from the royal residence in Lochau. The guests filled seven or eight tables.

On this visit Barnes had brought from Henry 500 gulden for Melanchthon and 50 for Luther. Barnes brought with him a book by Dr. Richard Sampson, Henry's dean of the chapel, on the king's supremacy, and a volume of sermons to show the Lutherans how evangelical the king was. Also Henry felt called on to admonish the Lutherans to remain firm and steadfast against the Antichrist!

Barnes also saw Duke George of Saxony and lodged a complaint against Cochlaeus, who had written a book against King Henry.

XI.
English Theologians at Wittenberg.

In November *"ille niger Anglicus*, that black English-man," as Luther called Barnes, was again in Wittenberg, and with other English delegates had conferences with the Lutherans about Henry's divorce.

On Sunday, Nov. 7, 1535, Luther had a famous interview with the papal nuntio, Peter Paul Vergerio, in the Wittenberg Castle. He wrote Jonas that with his character-istic speeches he also acted as the spokesman for Dr. Barnes, who had not gone to the Castle.

In December, Edward Fox, Bishop of Hereford, and Archdeacon Nicholas Heath appeared as Henry's ambas-sadors to treat more fully with the Lutherans.

They conferred with the Elector at Weimar on Dec. 9, and went with him to the meeting of the Protestant princes at Schmalkalden. There they delivered the King's message to the Saxon Chancellors Brueck and Burchart. Fox addressed the whole meeting and admonished the Protestants to unity, warned against the Anabaptists, discussed the papal preten-sions, and insisted on unity of doctrine before entering the council called by the pope.

The Schmalkaldeners rejoiced over Henry's readi-ness to agree with them in doctrine, and on Dec. 25 the Englishmen and the heads of the Bund signed a petition Henry might further the pure Gospel according to the Augsburg Confession and the Apology.

On Jan. 1, 1536, the Englishmen were in Wittenberg. "Luther lovingly embraces them and is even delighted by their courtesy," writes Melanchthon. The doctrines were discussed till some time in April. The Englishmen agreed with the Lutherans on the "Wittenberg Articles of 1536," subject to the approval of their King.

Luther joked about the importance attached to him by King Henry. After eleven universities had already given their decision, it seems the world will be lost "unless we poor beggars, the Wittenberg theologians, be heard."

While he will stand firmly by Katherine against Henry, "in other respects I will show myself not unfriendly towards them, in order that they may not think that we Germans are stone or wood."

He certainly was as good as his word. When reading these articles we are really amazed to see how far the peace-loving Luther was able to go in order to have peace and union with England, in spite of his former experiences with the old Harry. "It is indeed true, that we ought to have patience though everything in doctrine be not realized all at once, (as this has not occurred even among us)." So wrote Luther on April 20 to Vice Chancellor Burkhard, who translated into German the "Wittenberg Articles of 1536."

But the English King was playing the game of politics: he wanted the Lutherans to endorse his divorce. This they refused to do. Had they done so, England would have accepted the whole Augsburg Confession.

Owing to the meddling of the English King, the discussions came to naught. Luther was sorry for the waste of time and angry at the heavy expense to the Elector for the rich entertainment of the ambassadors.

Luther could not conceal his amazement at their seeming confidence in the justice of their cause. He was willing to listen to their arguments, but wearied of their persistent belaboring and prolonged stay, from December till April; and then they followed the Lutherans to the meeting of the Protestant princes at Frankfurt on April 24.

King Henry urged Philip of Hessen to urge Luther to favor Henry's divorce, but Luther did not know how to play politics, and he would not budge. He would not sacrifice his conviction for all England and the glory thereof. He, too, said, "Get thee behind me, Satan!"

On Saturday, Jan. 29, 1536, there was a disputation "Against the Private Mass." The Saxon Electoral Vice-Chancellor Francis Burkhard of Weimar took the floor several times. Bishop Fox also took part in the discussion. Luther spoke of the right, Christian manner in which princes were to get "private mass" from their court chaplains, and no doubt referred to Dr. Barnes, who had just been made King Henry's chaplain.

Melanchthon complained about the quibbling of the English: "They exercise me so that I can hardly breathe." He wrote Camerarius: "The Archdeacon, Nicholas Heath, is the only one of our guests who is distinguished by culture and learning; the rest are destitute of our philosophy and sweetness, so I avoid their society as much as I can." (Heath later became the powerful Archbishop of York.)

In May Fox wrote Frederick and signed himself, "*Electoralis Celsitudinis vestrac bonus amicus*—Your Electoral Highness' good friend." Strype writes the Germans thought this "without that sense of distance and good manners that became him."

Dr. Barnes returned to England in April or May, Bishop Fox arrived at the Convocation on July 4, and on the 11th laid before the House, "The Book of Articles of Faith and Ceremonies," which was greatly influenced by the "Wittenberg Articles."

In 1536 Edward Fox defended Alesius in a speech in which he said: "The Lay people do now know the Holy Scripture better than many of us. And the Germans have made the Text of the Bible so plain and easie by the Hebrew and Greek Tongues, that now many things may be better understood without any Glosses, at all, than by all the Commentaries of the Doctors. And moreover, they have so opened these Controversies by their Writings, that Women and Children may wonder at the blindness and Falsehood that hath been hitherto."

He, said this in reply to Bishop Stokesley of London, who sneered at the Word of God, which every cobbler was reading in his mother tongue.

"Who can refute a sneer?" asked Sidney Smith. From the above it seems some sneers can be refuted.

In the same Convocation "The right noble Lord Cromwell did defend the pure doctrine of the Gospel hard," writes Alesius. Cromwell presided at this meeting of the bishops, though there were two archbishops present.

"The Book of Articles of Faith" went over in part into the "Bishops' Book, The Institution of a Christian Man" of 1537. This was a triumph for the English Lutherans, and Bishop Fox had much to do with it; he was the chief advocate of the Lutheran doctrine. Parts of the "Bishops' Book" are nothing but parts of Luther's catechism. Froude calls the book "in point of language beyond all question the most beautiful composition that had as yet appeared in the English language."

Kaiser Karl's ambassador to England, Chapuys, places Fox with Cranmer and Thomas Cromwell "among the most perfect Lutherans in the world." Too bad this brilliant English Lutheran died in 1538.

After this mission Barnes remained in England for some time. When the Romanist Stephen Gardiner, Bishop of Winchester, had the ear of Henry, Barnes, in June of 1536, wrote Melanchthon not to come to England, as the King had repeatedly and earnestly invited him to do. In this year he also published at Wittenberg a History of the Lives of the Popes, dedicated to King Henry VIII. Luther furnished the "Introduction," in which he writes: "In the beginning, not being much versed in History, I attacked the Papacy *a priori*, i.e., from the Holy Scriptures. Now I am wonderfully delighted that others are doing the same *a posteriori*, i.e., from History. And since, as the light appears, I understand that the histories agree with the Scriptures. For what I have learned from St. Paul and Daniel as teachers, that the Pope is the adversary of God and of all, this history indicates with its very finger; pointing out not merely genus and species, but the very individual."

Barnes took the material for his book from Platina and other good Catholic historians. Fueter says:"Protestant historiography has received its program from the hand of Luther himself. Its first work appeared under the eyes of the Reformer, at Wittenberg, and with a preface by him." (Prof. Fuerbringer of St. Louis has a copy of this rare book.)

In 1445 [sic] Luther wrote an Introduction to"Papal Fidelity of Hadrian IV and Alexander III shown to Kaiser Friedrich Barbarossa." This booklet is a literal translation of part of Barnes' book; the translation and notes likely by Luther himself.

When Jacob Schenck and Philip Moth were made Licentiates of Theology, Luther presided at the disputation on Oct. 10, 1536. Dr. Robert Barnes took part in the discussion"On the Power of the Council," which Pope Paul III on

June 4, had called to Mantua for May 23, 1537. No doubt in view of the "honorable guests," the city council sent eight cans of Rhine wine and four quarts of must to the banquet in the "black cloister," Luther's house.

In 1537 John Rogers, chaplain of the English merchants at Antwerp, came to Wittenberg, studied German, and for the press of Hans Luft prepared his whole Bible. "It is chiefly remarkable for the excessive Lutheranism of its notes, in which it out-Tyndales Tyndale himself." It has "the character of a Lutheran manifesto."

Rogers was the first of Bloody Mary's martyrs— Monday, Feb. 4, 1555. "He has been burned alive for being a Lutheran; but he died persisting in his opinion," wrote Count Noailles, the French Ambassador at London.

Humphrey Monmouth, a London alderman, bought and studied the works of Luther, befriended Tyndale, became "a Scripture man," and left a bequest for preaching thirty sermons in place of saying thirty masses after his funeral. In 1537 Barnes became his executor.

The preachers received thirteen shillings and four pence for each sermon. Barnes preached some of these "to the glory of Christ and the testification of Monmouth's faith."

Bishop Latimer hears that Barnes preached a very good sermon in London today (July 15, 1537) with great moderation and temperance. "I pray God continue with him; for then I know no one man shall do more good." He had Barnes preach at Hartlebury, Worcester, and Evesham and writes Cromwell on Dec. 25, 1537: "Surely he is alone in handling of a piece of Scripture, and in setting forth of Christ he hath no fellow" and wishes the King might hear him.

In a letter to Bullinger, Richard Hilles calls Barnes, Gerrard, or Garret, and Jerome, "preachers of the Gospel, of no mean order," and writing to the same Bullinger, John Butler calls them "three of our best ministers."

On August 3, 1537, Melanchthon rejoices that Barnes is released from danger and begs Aepinus to salute him from Melanchthon and command him to remember his old friends.

Strype surmises Barnes had to flee to Ireland.

Barnes "adopts a secular habit" does not seem very important today, but in that day it was so important that the imperial ambassador Chapuys writes it to his master, Kaiser Karl V.

Another proof of Barnes' importance—"sent like an ambassador with ten horse unto the duke of Saxony, elector, in the matters of the Gospel." The learned Bishop of Winchester indulges in the silly sneer that Luther's religion permits a man to travel with ten horses.

Lauterbach writes under date of Nov. 4, 1538: "A certain Englishman, a learned man, sat at table, who did not understand the German language. Said Luther: 'I propose to you as teacher of German my wife, who is very eloquent. She can do it so well that therein she far surpasses me.'" This "certain Englishman," with whom Luther joked, is taken to be Dr. Barnes.

In 1538 he introduced the saying of Mass and the Te Deum in English. In 1539 he was on the Commission to try the Anabaptists.

XII.
The Lutheran Embassy in London.

On January 2, 1538, King Henry wrote a cordial letter to the Lutherans of Germany, hoping for an agreement in doctrine, and at the end of February sent Christopher Mount to the meeting of the Smalcald League at Brunswick, asking them to send the promised embassy. Francis Burkhard, Vice Chancellor of Saxony, George a Boyneburg, LL. D., a Hessian nobleman, and Frederick Myconius, Superintendent of Gotha, were sent. On May 12 Luther wrote a beautiful letter to Bishop Fox of Hereford, with whom he had been intimate, bespeaking a kind reception for the members of the embassy. He had died four days before.

On the same May 12, a retainer of John Thixtoll had arrived at Wittenberg and reported on the state of things in England.

When the Germans reached England in May, the King embraced them and greatly regretted the absence of Melanchthon. He appointed three bishops and four doctors to confer with the Lutherans, and assigned Dr. Barnes a place on the German side; Cranmer was the President. Henry himself took part in the discussion, for was he not "the learnedest prince in Europe?" On all the doctrinal articles of the Augsburg Confession there was full agreement, but when it came to the articles on the abuses in the church, the King again played politics. Cranmer wrote Cromwell, "I perceive that the bishops seek only an occasion to break the concord."

One of these enemies was Bishop Gardiner, another was Tunstall of Durham, the same who had refused a scholar's place to Tyndale.

The Germans also saw through Henry's game. My-conius wrote:"He wants nothing else than to sit as Antichrist in the temple of God, and that King Harry be Pope. The precious treasures, the rich income of the Church-these are Harry's Gospel." Had it not been for the meddling of the King a second time, England would have adopted the whole Augsburg Confession.

The conferences were held in Archbishop Cranmer's palace at Lambeth.

The Saxon Elector had treated the English ambassadors as it became their rank; how did the English King treat the German ambassadors? Cranmer writes:"As concernyng the Oratours of Germanye, I am advertised, that thei are very evill lodged where thei be: For besides the Multitude of Ratts, daily and nythly runnyng in their chambers, which is no small disquietness; the Kechyn standeth directly against their Parlar, where they dayly Dine and Supp; and by reason thereof, the House savoreth so yll, that it offendeth all Men that come into it." Yet, when the embassy left for home in September, 1538 the king was full of compliments. He presented three horses and a carriage to Francis Burkhard, the Saxon Vice Chancellor, and wrote to the Elector of his "most blameless friends, who have presented arguments so eminent in sound learning, wisdom, uncommon candor, and supreme devotion to Christian godliness, that their intercourse has been in the highest degree charming and agreeable to us, and we entertain the well-assured hope that, with God's assistance, fruit and success will follow the counsels that have been begun."

"Though they failed in their immediate object, yet to their visit may be traced the Lutheran, the Augustan complexion of a considerable part of the present Articles of the

Church of England," says Dixon. Froude holds the English authorities "preferred the incongruities of Anglicanism to a complete reformation; and a 'midge-madge' (as Lord Burleigh calls it) of contradictory formularies to the simplicity of the Protestant faith."

Through these discussions in Wittenberg in 1536 and in England in 1538 some of the Augsburg Confession flowed into the Forty-two Articles of Edward VI and into the Thirty-nine Articles of Elizabeth, and from the Episcopal creed into the Methodist creed.

Barnes had a dispute with Stephen Gardiner, the powerful Bishop of Winchester, over the question whether it is unchristian to sue another for debt. Cromwell defended Barnes against the charge of heresy.

XIII.
A Second Lutheran Embassy to England.

During the conferences between the Protestants and the Emperor at Frankfort, February to April, 1539, Christopher Mount and Thomas Paynel represented the English cause and proposed another embassy to England. The Lutherans were willing to do everything in their power to further the truth of the Gospel. Melanchthon wrote two elegant letters to Henry, one to Nicholas Heath, and another to Cranmer. Vice Chancellor Burkhard and Ludwig von Baumbach were sent to England. They arrived on April 23. On the 29th King Henry received them graciously and so did Cromwell on May 2. The Germans had high hopes of success.

Soon the King's politics changed again, and he was eager to be rid of the Lutherans. On May 16 and 18 there were fruitless interviews with Cromwell and others. On the 26th the Lutherans begged Henry to be guided alone by the truth of the Gospel, and the King made no attempt to conceal his anger. On the 31st the Lutherans went home. Forgeries were circulated in England to injure the Lutheran cause.

King Henry gave to Barnes, "*familiaris noster*, our household servant," a credence to King Christian III of Denmark and to the Elector John Frederick of Saxony. On May 12 Ambassador Barnes in a speech to King Christian said Henry VIII was "willing to join with Christians against the Papists for the preservation of the Christian religion."

Barnes persuaded the King of Denmark and the Elector John Frederick of Saxony to arrange for a joint embassy to England to treat of a political league to follow a theological agreement. But the discouraging report of Burckhard and Baumbach dampened the enthusiasm and Henry was told he was to send an ambassador if a league was to be treated of at all; they could not venture to visit England because of the enmity to the Gospel in that country.

On June 15 Melanchthon writes Matthew Delius to "reverently salute (Barnes) in the names of Luther, Jonas, and myself, and say that we long for his letters and wonder at the silence of the eloquent man."

XIV.
Fresh Persecutions.

"The bloody statute of the Six Articles,""the whipe with sixe strings" was to be enforced on July 12. To avoid the penalties, Archbishop Cranmer sent away his wife, a niece of

Andreas Osiander of Nuernberg. Hugh Latimer resigned his bishopric. Alesius fled to Wittenberg. Sent by Henry to Hamburg, Barnes dared not return for some time. Luther wrote: "The devil is driving this king, so that he vexes and martyrs Christ. . . . He is still the same King Harry whom I portrayed in my first book. ... He wants to kill the Pope's body but to keep his soul, i.e., his false doctrines."

Cranmer wrote a book against these papistic "Six Articles" and almost came losing his head; Cromwell saved him by forcing the book from the enemy.

On November 1st Melanchthon wrote Henry a long letter boldly and eloquently denouncing the Six Articles. Thomas Walpole later translated it, and Richard Grafton risked the publication, though he had spent six weeks in the Tower for printing Matthews' Bible.

The leaven was working. Sir Nicolas Carew, master of the king's horse and a knight of the garter, was executed March 3, 1539. When he was brought to the scaffold, he openly acknowledged his errors and superstitions in which he had formerly lived, and blessed God for his imprisonment; for he then began to relish the life and sweetness of God's holy Word, which was brought him by his keeper, one Phillips, who followed the Reformation, and had formerly suffered for it.

Myconius wrote: "Herod against Christ, and Nero against the Apostles, have not been so tyrannical. This kingdom has been well dyed and fertilised with the blood of Christians."

XV.
Henry Marries Anne of Cleves.

When the powerful Cardinal Wolsey fell from power, he said to Thomas Cromwell, in the words of Shakespeare: "Cromwell, I charge thee, fling away ambition.
....Be just and fear not.
Let all the ends thou aims't at be thy country's,
Thy God's, and truth's; then if thou falls't, 0 Cromwell,
Thou fall'st a blessed martyr."

Certainly one end he aimed at was his country's greatness. He freed England from the tyrannical rule of the pope. He became known as "The Hammer of the Monks" for suppressing many monasteries, which had become corrupt. Yes, corrupt. In 1516 Contarini, later Cardinal, wrote: "Unfortunately in some of the chief and celebrated cities most cloisters have become almost *lupanaria*"—houses of ill fame.

The immoral and infidel Bembo, Secretary to Pope Leo X and later Cardinal, said: "I have often found, under the affairs of friars, all human wickedness covered with diabolical hypocrisy." In 1536 the Pope's own commission wrote: "Many have departed from God to such an extent that they are a scandal to secular Christians and do much harm by their example. We think all the conventual orders ought to be abolished." The "standing army of the pope" was wholly disbanded in England. The Augsburg Confession and Melanchthon's Apology "translated by Richard Tavernier at the commandment of Lord Thomas Cromwell," were printed between 1536 and 1539. Cromwell licensed Coverdale's translation and spent 600 marks —$20,000—to have it printed in 1539, his coat of arms on the title-page.

This is Cromwell's Bible, or the Great Bible. He presented a copy to King Henry and ordered every parish in England to get one, so that the people could read it. In two letters Cranmer warmly thanks Cromwell for his efforts. He favored Gospel preachers, for Bishop Latimer wrote in 1538: "Your Lordship has promoted many more honest men since God promoted you than any of like authority have done before you." He protected men denounced by the infamous "Six Articles." He sought the friendship of the German Lutherans in order to defend England against a possible invasion by the Emperor Charles V and King Francis I of France.

The attempts of Thomas Cromwell to unite all Protestants seemed in a fair way to be successful; in order to cement the union, he planned the King's marriage with Anne of Cleves, the Saxon Elector's sister-in-law. Dr. Barnes was again sent to Germany to make the arrangements, and to comfort the Lutherans with the assurance that Henry had ceased persecuting the Protestants in England under the Six Articles. "There is no persecution," wrote John Butler in London to Bullinger, "the Word is powerfully preached by one Barnes and his fellow-ministers. Books of every kind may safely be exposed to sale."

When Barnes returned, Henry would not grant him a hearing, in spite of Cromwell's request. Though Barnes was no longer in favor, Cromwell promoted him to the prebend of Lanbedye.

This living was offered by Bishop Barlow of St. David's to Cromwell for one of his chaplains, "Dr. Barones not the unfaithfullest." It was "the onely best," eighteen pounds the year.

When Bishop Gardiner of Winchester objected to Barnes, a man defamed of heresy, being ambassador, Cromwell removed the powerful bishop from the Privy Council.

Though the Elector persistently advised against the marriage (and thereby incurred the enmity of his relatives), the marriage was arranged.

Henry was told Anne excelled the Duchess of Milan "as the golden sun did the silver moon." He sent Christopher Mont, or Mount, a German, and Beard, to look over Anne and her sister. On account of the high collars, much could not be seen of them, and the men misliked the German styles. They were asked: "Would you see them naked?" History does not record the reply. Henry would not rely upon description, he wanted pictures. Lucas Cranach was sick and could not paint. Henry sent his own court painter, Hans Holbein, to paint the portrait, which gave great satisfaction. Henry went secretly to Rochester to have a look at her, "to nurse love." He saw her looking through a window at a bull baiting. She was big, fat, homely, had "a brown complexion," could not speak English, had disagreeable habits, could not sing nor play an instrument; on the trip across she hurriedly learned to play cards; she was good at needle work. Needle work—for Henry VIII!!! "I like her not." "Is there no remedy but that I must needs put my neck in the yoke?" The King was shown by Cromwell there was no remedy, and the yoke was put on the royal neck on January 6, 1540.

"The sonday after there were kepte solempne Justes ... on whiche daie she was apparelled after the Englishe fassion, with a Frenche whode, whiche so set furth her beautie and good visage, that euvry creature reioysed to behold her." So says Hall, the English writer, thus agreeing with Sleidan, the German historian, who calls her "a virgin of elegant form."

There is no accounting for tastes, and the King no doubt thought—

"What care I how fair she be,

If she be not fair to me."

Henry blamed Cromwell for the whole miserable mess, and then promptly fell in love with pretty Katherine Howard.

XVI.
A Third Embassy to England.

On Thursday after Three Kings, Baumbach again arrived in London, and on Friday morning Cromwell only wanted to know had he power to form a political treaty. On Saturday Christopher Mont told Baumbach the King would receive him at Greenwich Sunday morning at nine. All Henry wanted to know was had Baumbach power to conclude a political treaty. On Tuesday, Jan. 12, Cromwell called Burckhard and Baumbach and told them the King wanted a political alliance first of all; the religious question could be settled later.

The Lutherans replied nothing could be done till they had agreed on religion. Burckhard said this in Latin and Baumbach in French.

Cromwell told the Lutherans he appreciated their religious convictions, but, as the world stood then, he would side with his king, and if he should die for it. He again advised to make the political treaty first and then agree on religion. And he begged them to speak becomingly and not hard with the king, so as not to make him ungracious and impatient.

Presently Baumbach was received by the king, who was angry at the firmness of the Lutherans and threw contempt on their usefulness as political allies.

On Jan. 21 Cromwell bade Baumbach farewell.

Franz Burckhard was sent to England in 1538, 1539, 1540, 1547, and 1559—"the finest orator to be had in Germany at this time," says Myconius.

Henry again wished to join the Bund of Schmalkalden, and on April 14, Melanchthon wrote a long letter for the Elector's use, saying, "if the king wished to enter the League for other reasons than those of religion, that this was entirely at variance with the principles of the League."

A conference between English and German theologians is suggested at any place the English king might choose. "For we greatly desire that true and godly agreement be established between the English and German Churches." With the letter went "Writing of the Wittenberg Theologians sent to the King of England."

It was love's labor lost.

On May 10 Cranmer tried to apologize for his king and begged the Lutherans to be patient.

Henry never lived with his fairy queen; he treated her brutally; on July 10 he repudiated her on the ground "that the king having married her against his will, he had not given a pure, inward and complete consent"; he formally divorced "the Flanders mare" on July 24. She agreed and lived happy ever after. This insured her life and a good living of 12,000 ducats per year.

On July 28 he chopped off the head of his minister Cromwell, who had engineered the marriage.

The King told Marillac, the French ambassador: "He wished by all possible means to lead back religion to the way of truth. Cromwell, as attached to the German Lutherans, had always favored the doctors who preached such erroneous opinions, and that recently, warned by some of his principal servants to reflect that he was working against the instructions of the King and the Act of Parliament, he said that the affair would soon be brought to such a pass that the King with all his power could not prevent it, but rather his own party would be so strong that he would make the King descend to the new doctrines even if he had to take arms against him."

XVII.
Barnes In Trouble.

The Romanists, headed by Stephen Gardiner, were again in power. On the first Sunday in Lent Gardiner preached at Paul's Cross and made severe remarks on the Lutheran doctrine of justification by faith and on "devils offering heaven without works to sinners."

Barnes felt this as a homethrust, and on mid-Lent Sunday from the same text attacked the Bishop's doctrine and also indulged in some personalities. He called Gardiner a fighting-cock and himself another, and challenged the bishop to trim his spurs for a battle. He taunted him with concealed Romanism. Barnes said if he and the bishop were at Rome together, much money would not save his life, but for the bishop there was no fear—a little entreatance would purchase favor enough for him.

Traheron writes Bullinger: "The bishop was ably answered by Dr. Barnes,... with the most gratifying and all but universal applause."

On March 7, 1540, the French Ambassador Marillac despatches home: "A great doctor of the law, called Barnes, principal preacher of the new doctrine, angrily threw his glove upon the people, as a defiance to the Bishop, against whom he would maintain what he had said to the death."

On May 21, 1540, Barnes wrote Aepinus, pastor at Hamburg:

"Write, I entreat you to Philip [Melanchthon] in my name, as soon as possible, that he come not hither before he receives a letter from me; for I would not have him exposed to danger by any reason of any hopes he builds upon me. For I have been deceived myself...

"A fierce controversy is going on between the bishop of London, Gardiner and myself, respecting justification by faith and purgatory. He holds that the blood of Christ cleanseth only from past sins previous to baptism; but that those committed since are blotted out partly by the merits of Christ, and partly by our own satisfactions. He adds too, that voluntary works are more excellent than the works of the ten commandments. As to purgatory, he says, that if a woman shall have caused masses to be celebrated, and shall have bestowed alms for the soul of her husband, she may boldly demand her soul on the day of judgment, and say that she has paid the price of his redemption. But I, on the other hand, in opposition to all these things, vindicate the efficacy of the blood of Jesus Christ my Lord; but hitherto I stand alone in doing it. For although many persons approve my statements, yet no one stands forward except Latimer. You shall hear the result of this controversy. . . . From the house of Thomas Parnell, to whom you will forward your letters.

"Yours from my heart,

R. B."

Gardiner complained to the king. Henry called in Barnes. They discussed merit, works, faith, free-will, grace. Barnes was willing to submit to the king.

"Yield not to me; I am a mortal man." He rose as he spoke, and turning to the sacrament, which stood on a private altar, and taking off his bonnet—"Yonder is the Master of us all; yield in truth to Him; otherwise submit yourself not to me."

Henry appointed two divines to hear the dispute in private and ordered Barnes to the Bishop's house for further instruction. When Gardiner asked Barnes to sign a recantation, Barnes left the house. Hearing this, the king was angry and ordered Barnes and his two friends, William Jerome and Thomas Garrett, to preach again in Easter week at St. Mary's Spital and publicly recant. Gardiner was present at Barnes' sermon, which was so unsatisfactory that the lord mayor appealed to the bishop whether Barnes should not at once be sent to prison. The sermons of the other two were equally unsatisfactory, and by order of the council all three were sent to the Tower. An act of attainder was passed against them in Parliament, and they were excepted from the general pardon, because they were "detestable heretics, who had conspired to set forth many heresies." On July 30, 1540, the three were drawn on a sledge through the middle of the streets to Smithfield and burned at one stake without so much as a hearing.

Garrett died with great courage, begging pardon for faults of rashness and vehemence. Cranmer in a letter to Cromwell calls Garrett a "forward and busy Lutheran."

At the same time the king killed three Catholics. No wonder people wondered what might be the king's religion. No wonder people wondered what they were to believe to save their necks.

XVIII.
Barnes Burnt.

When Dr. Barnes came to the stake he made a
confession of his faith to the people. He believed that our
Savior took His body from the Virgin Mary. He believed
alone in the work of Christ for our salvation, and not upon
good works, because they are always mixed with imperfec-
tions. Nevertheless, we must do good works because God
commands them, and to prove our faith, but not for any plea
of desert or merit. He believed the memory of the saints
ought be honored, but they ought not be prayed to, for we
have no warrant in the Bible for that.

He asked the sheriff for what false doctrine he was
to suffer death, but the sheriff did not know. He asked the
people if he had led any person into error by his preaching,
Receiving no answer, he said, "I understand I am condemned
for heresy by an act of Parliament. I pray God to forgive
all those who have been instrumental in this matter, and
particularly the Bishop of Winchester, if any way concerned."
Then he went on to pray for the king's prosperity, and that
his son, Prince Edward, might succeed him. Whereas he
had been reproached for preaching rebellion, he told them,
they were all bound to obey their King, not only for wrath,
but for conscience' sake.

Then he requested the sheriff to tell the king to
grant these five things:

First, That the lands taken by the king from the
monks might in part at least be given to relieve the poor;

Second, That the king would please take care that

marriage might be more honorably treated, and those engagements better performed; that men might not be permitted to part with their wives upon slight pretense, and then live scandalously with other women; and that the unmarried might not be permitted in licentious living;

Thirdly, That common swearers might be punished;

Fourthly, That the king advance the Reformation according to the Bible;

Fifthly, That the king be not imposed on by unorthodox preachers and ill counsel.

When this confession was attacked by one John Standish, who contemptuously called it "the doctrine of the Germans," Miles Coverdale nobly came out with a vigorous book in defense of his martyred friend and the slandered "doctrine of the Germans."

When Wittenberg heard of the burning of Barnes, the gentle Melanchthon piously wished an able tyrannicide might kill that monster Henry.

The confession of Barnes was published in German the same year, and Luther wrote an Introduction. In it he flays Henry, and erects a beautiful monument to "our good, pious table companion and guest of our home ... this holy martyr, St. Robertus."*

---

* The German title is *Bekantnus des Glaubens, die Robertus Barns der Heiligen Schrifft Doctor (im Deudschem Lande D. Antonius genent) zu Lunden im Engelland gethan hat, Anno MDXL, am xxx tag es Monats Julii, Da er zum Fewer one urteil und recht, unschuldig, unverhoerter sach, gefurt und verbrent worden ist. Aus der Englischen spracli verdeudscht. Mit einer Vorrhede D. Martini Luthers. Wittemberg, 1540.* Dr. Preserved Smith saw the copy in the British Museum.

"The patrearcke of Garmyne, Marten Luther," as
George Everat called him in the Privy Council, sang Dido's
farewell to life as the Queen of Carthage burnt herself, and
said to Mathesius: "That is a death song for Robert Barnes."
Here it is, as translated from Vergil by John Conington,
Professor of Latin at Oxford—
"Sweet relics of a time of love,
          When Fate and Heaven were kind,
Receive my life-blood, and remove
          These torments of the mind.
My life is lived, and I have played
          The part that Fortune gave.
And now I pass, a queenly shade,
          Majestic to the grave.
A glorious city I have built,
          Have seen my walls ascend,
Chastised for blood of husband spilt
          A brother, yet no friend.
Blest lot! yet lacked one blessing more,
          That Troy had never touched my shore."
Then, as she kissed the darling bed,
          "To die! and unrevenged!" she said,
"Yet let me die: thus, thus I go
          Rejoicing to the shades below.
Let the false Dardan feel the blaze
          That burns me pouring on his gaze,
And bear along, to cheer his way,
          The funeral presage of to-day."
          "The poor well feeleth the burning of Dr. Barnes
and his fellows which labored in the vineyard of the Lord,"
wrote Henry Brynklow in "The Lamentacyon of a Christen
Agaynst the Cytye of London," printed in 1545. In 1551

Roger Ascham, "The Scholemaster" of Queen Elizabeth, sent greetings to Bucer and "mine hostes Barnes," likely the widow of our martyr.

John Sastrow, a young scholar of Luebeck, published *Epicedion Martyris Christi, D. Roberti Barnes, Angli,* in which he compared King Henry to Busiris, the king of Egypt who sacrificed a stranger every year.

The tender feelings of the King were hurt, and he demanded satisfaction. The good Luebeckers excused the poet on the ground of his youth, but banished John Balhorn, the printer. The King had satisfaction, and soon Balhorn had the satisfaction of returning.

Youth was no excuse in the eyes of Bishop Bonner. He burned or hanged Richard Mechins, a boy of fifteen, for "participating in the heresies of Robert Barnes."

In 1555 Queen Mary condemned the writings of Barnes as heretical.

In 1573 John Day set forth "The Whole Works of Tyndal, Frith, and Dr. Barnes in one tome"; it was edited by John Fox.

King Henry again needed the help of the Germans. In November, 1544 he sent Walter Bucler and Christopher Mount to the continent. In February, 1545, he wrote himself, offering Mary or Elizabeth to the Duke of Holstein and protesting "that ther is no Prince nor man in the woorlde that desyreth more the glorye of God, and meaneth setting furth of His Woord than we do."

He was refused by the Bund of Schmalkalden at Frankfort in January, 1546.

In May, 1546, Henry sent John Masone to Heidelberg to offer Mary to Duke Philip, nephew of Frederick II, Elector of the Pfalz, who had lately turned Lutheran. The

German Elector refused the English King.

The King would make more concessions to form "The League Christian."

The Smalcald war broke out in the summer of 1546, and on January 28, 1547, came the end of Henry VIII.